FANTASTIC FLIGHT TO FREEDOM

FANTASTIC FLIGHT TO FREEDOM

Roger Schachtel

Illustrated by Charles Shaw

RAINTREE PUBLISHERS

Milwaukee • Toronto • Melbourne • London

Copyright © 1980, Raintree Publishers Inc.

All rights reserved. No part of this book may be reproduced
or utilized in any form or by any means, electronic or mechanical,
including photocopying, recording, or by any information storage
and retrieval system, without permission in writing from the
Publisher. Inquiries should be addressed to Raintree Publishers Inc.,
205 West Highland Avenue, Milwaukee, Wisconsin 53203.

Library of Congress Number: 79-23116

2 3 4 5 6 7 8 9 0 84 83 82 81

Printed and bound in the United States of America.

Library of Congress Cataloging in Publication Data

Schachtel, Roger.
Fantastic flight to freedom.

SUMMARY: Relates the experiences of two teenage
boys who decide to escape from Castro's Cuba by stowing
away in the landing gear of an airplane.
1. Cuba—History—1959-   —Juvenile literature.
2. Ramirez, Armando Socarras—Juvenile literature.
3. Refugees, Political—Cuba—Biography—Juvenile
literature.   4. Refugees, Political—United States—
Biography—Juvenile literature.   [1. Refugees,
Political.   2. Cuba—History—1959-   3. Survival]
I. Shaw, Charles, 1941-   II. Title.
F1788.S385   972.91'064   79-23116
ISBN 0-8172-1551-4 lib. bdg.

CONTENTS

CHAPTER 1

A Piece of Rope and a Wheel

The fantastic flight to freedom of Armando Ramirez began on the afternoon of June 3, 1969. Two teenaged boys lay sprawled on their stomachs in a field of tall grass. The field bordered a runway at the José Marti Airport in Havana, Cuba. The two boys hoped that their hiding place was a secret to everyone but themselves. They lay as close to the earth as they could, pressing the palms of their hands tightly against the bent stalks of grass that broke through the warm earth. Although the day was not terribly hot and they were dressed lightly, the boys were perspiring heavily. They breathed quickly, as if they had just completed a difficult exercise.

In fact, the boys had been lying there for forty-five minutes. Their heavy perspiration and quick breathing were not signs of physical exertion. They were signs of fear—fear that their

hiding place would be discovered. But there was even greater fear of what the next few hours might bring. The boys seemed to hang on to the earth with their knotted fists as if they wanted to anchor themselves to it. But their determination to go through with their plan was greater than their fear of the unknown future.

The boys need not have worried about their hiding place being discovered. They had gotten onto the grounds of the airport without attracting any attention, although many guards were on patrol. And none of their family or friends knew that the boys were here. But within a day, everyone in the world who read a newspaper or listened to a news broadcast would know that they had been there.

The runway a few feet away from the boys was the place where planes slowly taxi to before takeoff. They stop there for a few minutes before picking up speed and taking off. Every so often one of the boys would cautiously raise his head just a few inches from the ground. Slowly, he would part the blades of grass which blocked his view of the runway. He would watch the DC-8 at the far end of the runway that was preparing for flight. Surrounded by a group of mechanics and crew members, it was now taking on cargo, baggage, and passengers. Even at this distance it wasn't hard to figure out the job of everyone who was working on the jet.

The boy noticed two of the mechanics looking inside the well into which the wheels are pulled once the plane is in flight. Abruptly, he nudged his companion.

"Jorge, they're looking inside the wheel well. Two of them! I hope nothing is wrong," he whispered.

The 145 passengers boarding the DC-8 at the same time that the two boys were hiding in the grass were all leaving their homes in Cuba for Madrid, Spain.

The revolutionary government which had taken over Cuba in 1959 had cut back on emigration. So there were very few planes leaving Cuba every week, but there were tens of thousands of people on waiting lists who wanted seats on these planes.

And all these people were determined to get away from Cuba even though, in most cases, they would have to leave loved ones behind.

And there were thousands of others who would have gone on the waiting lists and put up with all of these hardships to get away. But the price of a ticket was simply more than they could afford.

From the José Marti Airport near Havana, a few planes left weekly for Spain and Mexico. From the airport near Varadero Beach, there were two flights every day to Miami. Even with flights leaving so rarely, about 500,000 Cubans had managed to leave the country in the ten years following the revolution. Those who were determined to leave Cuba were driven by a fierce will.

Finally, on the afternoon of June 3, 1969, flight 904 from Havana to Madrid was ready to board. The 145 people who had been lucky enough to have tickets were led to the foot of the ramp going up into the plane. Two stewardesses stood at the top of the ramp to take tickets and show them to their seats.

Now the passengers were all seated inside the plane. The ramp was taken away and the door to the plane was locked into place. Slowly the plane taxied to the end of the runway. Inside, a cheerful stewardess gave instructions about seatbelts and oxygen masks. The engines began to rev up for takeoff.

In the last moments on the ground, as the four

engines roared, a stewardess happened to glance out the window. She noticed two boys in their teens running toward the plane. Each was carrying a piece of rope. She wondered if they were trouble makers, or just kids who had somehow found a way into the airport and were enjoying a forbidden expedition. Only a few seconds later the DC-8 began its rapid sprint down the runway. Then its wheels left the earth. The jet was airborne, en route to Madrid. What no one inside the plane knew at the time was that two additional passengers were clinging to its belly!

CHAPTER 2

In the Well of Darkness

The plan that Armando Socarras Ramirez and Jorge Péres Blanco had dreamed up in order to get away from Cuba seemed crazy, desperate, and hopeless. But they were determined to escape, and they couldn't think of any other way. They had only met recently at a baseball game. Their first talk together had soon turned to their desire to live somewhere else. Each wanted more than anything to leave a life of rules and regulations where they had few choices about how they played or where they worked. And there was something else. Jorge was sixteen years old and Armando was seventeen, and they would soon face three dangerous years of military service.

One day the boys had bicycled to the airport. They wanted to see if it was possible to hide on an airplane leaving for the free world. They cycled slowly around the wire fence that surrounded most of the grounds. Finally they discovered a small piece of the fence that someone else had dug under. The boys left their bikes nearby and crawled underneath the sharp, twisted ends of the barbed wire.

Then they had crawled through the tall grass to the edge of the runway, which stood only a few hundred feet away, and watched a jet taking off. Only seconds after the plane left the earth, the boys saw its wheels being lifted into a compartment. The doors were then shut under the compartment so that the wheels, now locked inside, could no longer be seen. Armando and Jorge looked at each other in triumph. They had found their private seats on a jet leaving Havana! They would travel in that dark compartment housing

the wheels. All that remained was for them to set a date.

———————

And now, on June 3, 1969, the boys watched from their hiding place in the grass as the jet slowly came toward them. They knew that the plane would stop for only about thirty seconds at the place where it briefly rested before taking off. They would have very little time to run to the wheels, scramble up them, and somehow get inside the wheel well.

The plane inched to a stop just fifty feet from where they crouched. Each boy clutched at the piece of rope he planned to use to tie himself to some pipe or machinery inside the wheel well. The plan was for the boys to count to ten once the plane had stopped. Then they would run out, climb the wheels, and get inside. Of course, they didn't really know how much room they'd have in there, or what they'd tie themselves to.

Finally the moment of truth arrived. The plane's engines were briefly silenced, while the pilot prepared to turn on all the power needed to get the jet off the ground. The boys counted to ten. They were both amazed that it was happening and they *were* going through with it.

In what seemed like an instant each boy heard his own voice and the voice of his friend speak the number ten. Armando and Jorge ran to the plane as fast as they could.

16

Jorge reached the wheels just before Armando did. He climbed up them, hoisting himself up into the wheel well. Just a glance into the well told Armando that it would be impossible for him to find a place in there with his friend. The inside was so crowded with machinery, that Armando couldn't even see where there would be room for the wheels once they were lifted inside!

Armando ran over to the other set of wheels, jumped on top of them, and hoisted himself into the well.

Barely a second after Armando had wrapped his arms and legs around the machinery, the engines were turned on and the plane sped down the runway. Armando had never felt such a sensation of speed before! He only looked down for a second—the sight of the airstrip rushing by underneath was too frightening. It made him dizzy.

Suddenly Armando could feel the wheels lifting off the ground. He held on to his steel nest with a grip that was as strong as his desire to go on living. More and more space separated him from the earth as the plane climbed, and he prayed for the moment when the wheels would be lifted up and the doors closed. A few seconds later, he felt the wheels begin to move toward him, and he even permitted himself a smile of relief. But the smile turned into a look of horror as the wheels brushed against his back and burned him with the heat caused by their rolling on the runway.

Armando pressed himself more and more tightly against the machinery he was holding on to. The wheels continued to rise higher, pressing more and more tightly against him. His fear of being burned was quickly taken over by the fear that he would be crushed! He took his feet from the tubing they were wrapped around and began to kick at the wheels. But his struggle against the plane's machinery was hopeless.

And then, just when Armando had given up hope, the wheels stopped moving and locked into place. His eyes were not used to the total darkness, and he could see nothing. But he was amazed by the noise of the four turbofan engines. The cotton he had stuffed into his ears gave almost no protection against the jet's roar. He wondered if he could live through eight more hours of this. A full 5,500 miles separated Havana from Madrid. Armando realized with a shock that he hadn't had time to tie himself to anything. He must have dropped his piece of rope in the excitement of entering the wheel well. It seemed that he would have to depend on his own arms and legs to keep himself from falling out of the well if the bottom doors should open.

That thought had just crossed his mind when Armando felt the wheels begin to move slightly away from him. And then, disbelieving, he saw

that the wheel well was becoming brighter. The doors were opening, and the wheels began to drop out again! Did they know he was there? Was the pilot going to go back to Havana to have him and Jorge arrested? Or was the pilot just planning to get rid of his unwanted human cargo by dropping it into the ocean? Armando turned his head

to look below. He could see the ocean thousands of feet beneath him. Nothing at all separated him from it. He pressed his eyes tightly shut and vowed to hold on for as long as he had to.

Inside the airplane the passengers were relaxing after the excitement of taking off. Once the wheels had been lifted back into the plane, there was a lot less noise. The jet seemed to fly more smoothly, too. But then, suddenly, a jolt shook the aircraft. It began to waver and tremble, and the people heard a grinding noise. Some of the passengers who had never been in an airplane before did not realize that the wheels were being lowered a second time. They asked the stewardess to find out why it was happening.

The noise had already stopped when the

stewardess entered the cockpit a few minutes later.

"Some of the passengers want to know why the wheels had to be lowered a second time," the stewardess asked the captain.

"Oh, it's nothing to be worried about," the captain answered. "The landing gear didn't seem to fit back in properly. Maybe something got stuck in there during takeoff. So I pulled the wheels out and put them back in again. Whatever might have been in there isn't in there anymore."

CHAPTER 3

Life Before the Flight

But the captain was wrong about what had been inside the wheel well. Armando was still there. His determination to save himself and start a new life away from Cuba had kept his grip secure. He twisted his arms and legs tightly around the piping that was his only link with life. The doors to the wheel well stayed open for only a couple of minutes. But Armando did not know that the captain was satisfied that nothing remained in the well. As far as the boy was concerned, those doors could open again at any moment during the next eight hours. Without his rope tying him to the plane, the only security he could count on was his own arms and legs. In the hour remaining before he lost consciousness Armando lived over and over again those terrifying moments when the ground had opened up beneath him. Without relaxing his hold he managed to reach inside his sport shirt and take out a candy bar and some aspirin.

At least the opening of the doors had given Armando a bit of light. He was able to see where he could squeeze his five-foot-four-inch frame so that he would not feel so pressed by the wheels once they were pulled back into the plane. But the opening of the doors also let cold air into the well. Soon the plane would reach 29,000 feet. The outside temperature would fall to forty-one degrees below zero! And Armando was only wearing a sports shirt and slacks.

To make matters worse, oxygen was becoming more and more scarce as the plane gained altitude.

For the first time since the plane had left the ground Armando began to wonder about Jorge, his friend in the other wheel well. Jorge was a year younger than Armando, and Armando felt protective toward him. He wondered if Jorge had been prepared for the second opening of the well. Armando could not bear to think of what might have happened to his friend.

As the amount of oxygen grew smaller and smaller, Armando began to feel giddy and faint. He tried to keep his mind active by looking back on his life in Cuba, recalling what had driven him to risk his life to get off the island. The more he remembered, the less he regretted his immediate danger.

When he was not away at school, Armando lived with his parents, four brothers, a sister, and three other family members in one large room in Havana. Overcrowded housing was a fact of life for most Cubans, even before the 1959 Revolution. At least Fidel Castro and his fellow revolutionary leaders had torn down the worst slums of Havana. They had been rows of tin-walled shacks without electricity or water, and disease was everywhere.

Unfortunately not enough new housing had been built for the people made homeless after the revolution. So there were many more people to

crowd into the houses which were allowd to stand. And the problem was made even worse by a large population increase—more than 150,000 people a year—on an island which had only held six million people in 1959. The waiting lists for new apartments were hopelessly long and kept growing longer. And large groups of people were forced to live in small spaces.

But the crowded housing and the rationing of food, which had also followed the revolution, were not the only reasons why Armando decided to leave Cuba. Armando could not foresee a desirable future for himself there. He knew that he would have very little control over the course of his education or job. And Armando had a fierce ambition to become an artist. This, he knew, would almost certainly not be possible in Cuba.

A year before Armando's flight to Madrid, the Cuban government had decided that he should be trained as a welder. He had been sent to a vocational school in a small village surroundedd by fields of sugarcane. Armando and his fellow students had spent as much time cutting cane as they spent studying welding and other crafts.

Armando also knew that, even if he were lucky enough to paint as a hobby and his work was of professional quality, it would be almost impossible for him to sell anything if it did not celebrate the Cuban Revolution. After all, the government had control over which paintings were shown and which books were published in Cuba. Almost ten years after Armando left the island the laws would be changed so that painters could sell their work privately. But in 1969 there was no sign that this would every happen.

All Armando could see in the future for himself was vocational training for a job he had not chosen, followed by three years of military service that might cost him his life. And throughout the vocational training and the military service he would spend long periods of time in the sugar fields, cutting the stalks of sugarcane in the burning sun. No, such a life was not for him.

Armando Socarras Ramirez was inside the wheel well of a jet traveling at 29,000 feet because he preferred the possibility of death to the certainty of life without individual freedom.

CHAPTER 4

Some Wanted to Stay

Of course, not everyone living in Cuba felt like Armando. A great many Cubans would have thought the loss of their individual freedom was a price they were willing to pay for the changes which Fidel Castro's government had brought about in their country. It would be wrong, in telling of Armando's adventure, not to state the case for those Cubans who gladly chose to stay at home. It is by no means true that all Cubans were desperate to flee their country. Most older Cubans probably felt that the only freedom they had enjoyed under Fulgencio Batista, the man Castro drove out in 1959, was the freedom to be poor, illiterate, and without medical care.

The most powerful politician in Cuba for the twenty-five years before the 1959 Revolution was Fulgencio Batista, who served as elected president in the early 1940s. In 1952, Batista took over the government with a military coup.

There had always been unemployment and poverty in Cuba. But Cuba's problems got even worse under Batista's dictatorship. Poverty in the countryside was widespread. The government completely ignored the peasants living in the country. They could not read or write, and disease was widespread. Except for the sugar industry, the Cuban economy was not developed. Organized crime took over many businesses in Havana, the capital of the country. Blacks were discriminated against for certain jobs. They were even forbidden to enter some public parks. The police used brutality against Batista's political enemies every day.

Even his enemies admit that Fidel Castro's fight against Batista was heroic. The last part of the struggle began in 1956. Fidel Castro, then in exile, came back to Cuba with a tiny group of followers. They hid out in the Sierra Maestra Mountains, promising to overthrow and replace Batista. Castro's forces grew larger as time passed. Castro finally entered Havana triumphantly on New Year's Day, 1959, just after Batista had fled the country. Castro had promised to hold free elections, but he did not keep his promise. Instead, he took over the government himself. Still, most Cubans welcomed the change, because they had hated and feared Batista so much.

Many of the things Castro did during the first years of his rule pleased the Cubans even more. Unemployment fell amost to zero. Illiteracy was reduced to four percent in 1961, when schools were closed for eight months so that 250,000 adults and teenagers could go to the rural areas and teach the peasants how to read. There were also great gains in health care. The rate of tuberculosis dropped seventy-five percent. Polio and diptheria were almost wiped out.

Castro cut city rents in half. He lowered the telephone and electricity rates and the price of medicine. He got rid of discrimination against non-whites. And he won respect from his people when he crushed the American-backed group of

Cuban exiles who tried to invade the island at the Bay of Pigs in 1962.

But there was a price the people paid for the revolution, too. Goods were scarce. The government had more say over what people did for a living, and even over what they read.

And so, while many people supported the revolution, many others decided to leave. There were many ways that people tried to flee the island. Great numbers faced danger in their effort to escape.

But none faced as much danger as young Armando Ramirez in his eight-hour ordeal high above the ocean in the belly of a jet plane.

CHAPTER 5

Quick, Get an Ambulance

During the first hour in the air Armando was slowly losing consciousness. His body could not keep going in the freezing cold and the limited oxygen at 29,000 feet. At that height there was only about half the oxygen Armando was used to. He tried to stay conscious by thinking about the people he loved whom he had left behind in Cuba—his parents, his brothers and sisters, his girlfriend.

None of them, of course, had any idea where he now was. None of them knew about the danger he was putting himself through. Armando wished he had been able to tell them his plans. But he knew that they would have been too terrified for his sake. They would have done anything to talk him out of his idea.

Knowing that his loved ones knew nothing about his crazy adventure made Armando feel that much more lonely as he huddled inside the wheel well, where it was colder than the freezer compartment of a refrigerator. Would he ever see his loved ones again?

Crystals of ice began to coat Armando's thin shirt and pants. For a short while he could feel little ice crystals inside his ears—forming around the little balls of cotton he had hoped would protect him from the noise. Armando couldn't see anything inside the wheel well. Actually, he was lucky he couldn't see, since he might have panicked if he had been able to observe some of the changes that were taking place on his body. The freezing cold would have made him numb to the pains in his joints and the itching on his skin which are standard symptoms of decompression sickness that comes from reduced air pressure. However, even a little light would have shown him that his arms and hands were swelling, and that splotches of blue discolored his skin.

Decompression sickness must have made Armando imagine that flashes of light were exploding in front of his eyes even in the darkness. Finally, a spell of extreme dizziness made him lose consciousness. In the hours that followed, his light clothing froze to his body. But Armando was beyond suffering. How he kept his hold on the little perch in the wheel well while unconscious for the last seven hours in the air is a mystery that Armando himself could only guess the answer to.

———

The flight went on smoothly as the plane headed east toward Madrid. Those nervous passengers who had never flown before were soon put at ease by the tranquility of jet travel in good weather. They had no sense of the huge plane hurtling

forward at 700 miles an hour. In fact, they had less sensation of speed than they would have had in an automobile moving at 50 miles an hour. The passenger section was kept at a comfortable temperature, and the stewardesses saw to it that all their needs were looked after. And that included two meals—dinner and breakfast! Most of the passengers were relaxed enough to sleep for a couple of hours as they sat in their seats. And they were delighted when they awoke to find landing time was that much closer.

Flying in a commercial jet as a regular passenger was quite a different matter than flying as a stowaway in an unpressurized and freezing wheel well!

The sun was setting in a clear sky as the plane approached the airport in Madrid. The plane began to lose altitude as the captain prepared for

landing. When the jet was only a few thousand feet from the ground the wheels were lowered. The captain reduced the speed of the plane to 140 miles per hour. In a few minutes the wheels touched the runway at Barajas Airport. Soon, the jet came to a halt and moved to the gate where the passengers would get off.

After the plane had emptied, the captain, the first officer, and the flight engineer walked down the ramp to the runway. They were supposed to wait for a car to pick them up and drive them into Madrid. Suddenly, they heard shouting coming from the center section of the plane. They ran over to where a group of mechanics were standing.

A crowd was gathering around the mechanics. As he got closer, the captain could see a security guard leaning over a bundle that looked like a dead body. Except that this body was moaning! It was a low moan that seemed to come from beyond the grave. The captain elbowed his way to the center of the crowd. He looked down at the body on the runway, hardly believing what his eyes were seeing.

There was Armando, lying underneath the wheel well. He had fallen out only a minute before, after the plane had come to a halt. Ice covered the boy's face and hands. His skin had turned light blue.

The security guard who was bent over the body looked up at the captain. He shook his head slowly and said, "He's alive! This kid was in the air with you hidden in the wheel well. And he's still alive! I saw him fall right out of the plane."

It didn't seem possible. But there was the boy, almost frozen, but alive. The shaken captain quickly regained control of himself and shouted, "An ambulance. Quick, get an ambulance!"

CHAPTER 6

A New Home, a New Life

Armando was taken to the Gran Hospital de la Beneficencia in the heart of Madrid. His temperature was 93.2 degrees, more than five degrees below normal! His pulse was also very weak——but he was alive. He responded quickly to the return to a normal life. Soon after arriving at the hospital, Armando regained consciousness for a short time. His first questions—after asking where he was—were about Jorge. What had happened to his partner in this great adventure?

The people at the hospital had no idea who Jorge was. He might have been a friend, a brother, or the patient himself, for all they knew. But the whole story was slowly pieced together as Armando got better.

At first Armando was dazed and confused. Upon being questioned, he first thought that he was in the *same* wheel well with Jorge. His unclear memory led him to tell the doctors that Jorge had been with him through most of the flight. Perhaps he wished so hard that this had been true that his memory changed the facts.

Reporters concluded that Jorge must have fallen out of the wheel well and been killed the first time the captain had lowered the wheels, just after leaving Havana. Then it was decided that Jorge must have been killed when the captain lowered the wheels before arriving in Madrid.

But as Armando's memory cleared in the following weeks and he remembered getting into a different wheel well from Jorge's, it was thought that Jorge might not have been quick enough in climbing into his own wheel well. A blast from the jet engines might have knocked him over before the plane took off. In that case he would probably still be in Cuba now. But the Cuban authorities did not give any information about Jorge to the wondering world.

And the world *was* wondering. Armando and Jorge had captured the imaginations of the people everywhere. The day after Armando got to Madrid the story of his daring flight from Cuba found a place on the front pages of the world's major newspapers. Some news photographers were allowed to take pictures of him in his hospital bed.

What amazed everyone who heard the

story—apart from the incredible courage of the two stowaways—was the medical mystery of Armando's survival. For one thing, the chief engineer of the company that made the DC-8 said that there was only one chance in a million that the wheels wouldn't crush someone hiding in the wheel well. But even so, how did the boy live through the lack of oxygen, the low pressure, and a temperature of 40 degrees below zero?

The best explanation that was given for Armando's survival was that his body temperature may have fallen at just the right pace to adjust to the decrease in oxygen. The body needs less oxygen as its temperature gets lower. If the tempera-

ture drops too quickly, then the body will freeze and die. As one doctor who was talking about Armando put it, "If he had been chilled too fast, he would have died. But through gradual cooling his body's need for oxygen could have kept up with the supply."

Still, this explanation was only a guess. It did not explain why Armando did not die from other things that usually happen to people who are unprotected at such high altitudes. There was simply no theory that explained exactly how Armando survived.

———————

Only a few days after he got to Madrid, Armando was already thinking about his future. He had never wanted to live in Spain. His goal had always been to go to America, where he had some uncles who lived in New Jersey. To him, America was the land of opportunity, where he had the best hope of living his life in his own way. The only reason he had stowed away on a jet headed for Spain was that he did not live close to the airport from which planes for Miami took off.

Armando could not remember exactly where his American relatives lived. However, his adventure had gotten so much publicity that one of his uncles phoned him in Madrid and invited Armando to live with him in Passaic, New Jersey. An American organization called the International Rescue Committee arranged for Armando to fly to New York and join his uncle.

On July 25, 1969, seven weeks after stowing away in the wheel well of the *DC-8*, Armando Socarras Ramirez boarded a jet—this time as a regular passenger—and flew from Madrid to New York. The difference between the trip to New York and the journey in the wheel well the month before greatly amused Armando. This time he enjoyed the luxury of jet travel as it was meant to be enjoyed.

But, as he leaned back in his soft seat, he also felt humble and grateful. And his joy was touched with sadness when he remembered the friend who had not been as lucky as he. He promised himself that he would prove worthy of the great opportunity to live in the United States. This was the reward for his courage—and Jorge's courage, too. For he doubted that he would have been brave enough to do what he did if he had started alone. If he hadn't had Jorge to plan with and share his fears with, he would probably still be in Cuba.

When Armando got to New York he was met by a group of reporters, as well as by his uncle Elo Fernandez. The reporters questioned him about his reasons for risking his life to flee Cuba. Armando's answer was brief and direct.

"There was no future at all for me. I was look-

ing for a new world and a new future. If I was in the same situation, I would do it again."

Cuba had lost a young man of courage and determination. America had gained a citizen in this seventeen-year-old hero whose fantastic flight to freedom amazed the world with an incredible tale of survival in the air.